A Pet's Life

Rabbits

Anita Ganeri

Heinemann Library
Chicago, Illinois

Design by Richard Parker and Tinstar Design Limited (www.tinstar.co.uk)
Originated by Dot Gradations
Printed and bound in China by South China Printing Company

07 06 05
10 9 8 7 6 5 4 3

**Library of Congress
Cataloging-in-Publication Data**
Ganeri, Anita, 1961-
   Rabbits / Anita Ganeri.
      v. cm. -- (A pet's life) (Heinemann first library)
Includes bibliographical references and index.
Contents: What is a rabbit? -- Rabbit babies -- Your pet rabbit -- Choosing your rabbit -- Setting up your cage -- Rabbit play-time -- Welcome home -- Feeding time -- Cleaning the cage -- Growing up -- A healthy rabbit -- Old age.
   ISBN 1-4034-3995-8 (Hardcover) -- ISBN 1-4034-4274-6 (pbk.)
   1. Rabbits--Juvenile literature. [1. Rabbits as pets. 2. Pets.] I. Title. II. Series.
   SF453.2.G36 2003
   636.9'322--dc21

2002151593

Acknowledgments
The author and publishers are grateful to the following for permission to reproduce copyright material: pp. 4 RSPCA/E. A. Janes; pp. 5, 6 John Daniels; pp. 7, 12 Chris Honeywell; pp. 8, 9, 13, 14, 15, 16, 17, 18, 19, 20, 21, 24, 25, 27 Tudor Photography; pp. 10, 11, 22, 23 Warren Photographic/Jane Burton; p. 26 Ardea/Johan D. Meester.

Cover photograph reproduced with permission of Alamy/Martin Ruegner.

The publishers would like to thank Jacque Schultz, CPDT, Lila Miller, DVM, and Stephen Zawistowski, Ph.D., CAAB of the ASPCA™ for their assistance in the preparation of this book.

Also, special thanks to expert reader, Dr. Roberta Drell, Morton Grove Animal Hospital, Morton Grove, Illinois.

Every effort has been made to contact copyright holders of any material reproduced in this book. Any omissions will be rectified in subsequent printings if notice is given to the publisher.

ASPCA™ and The American Society for the Prevention of Cruelty to Animals™ are registered trademarks of The American Society for the Prevention of Cruelty to Animals.

Some words are shown in bold, **like this.** You can find out what they mean by looking in the glossary.

Contents

What Is a Rabbit?

Rabbits are very popular pets. They come in lots of colors, from black to golden brown. There are many different sizes of rabbits, from tiny to large.

Small rabbits, like these Netherland dwarves, are good for beginning rabbit owners.

Here you can see the different parts of a rabbit's body and what each part is used for.

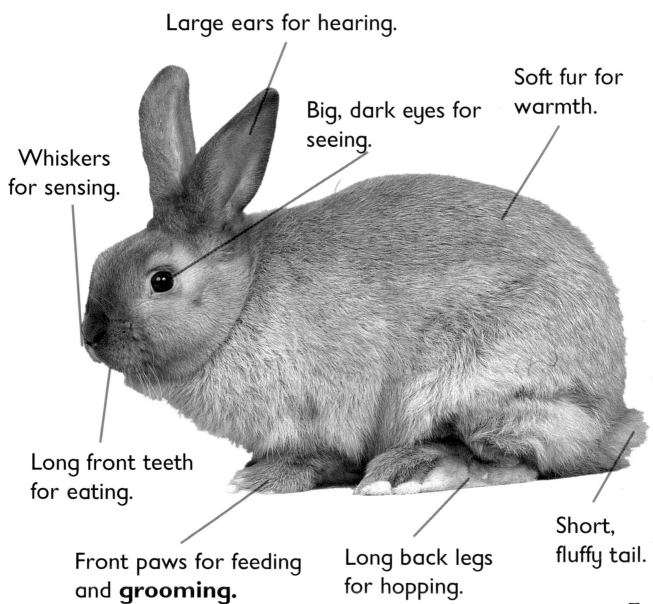

Large ears for hearing.

Big, dark eyes for seeing.

Soft fur for warmth.

Whiskers for sensing.

Long front teeth for eating.

Front paws for feeding and **grooming.**

Long back legs for hopping.

Short, fluffy tail.

Rabbit Babies

Baby rabbits are called kits. They are born with no fur and with their eyes closed. A mother rabbit may have as many as eight babies in a **litter.**

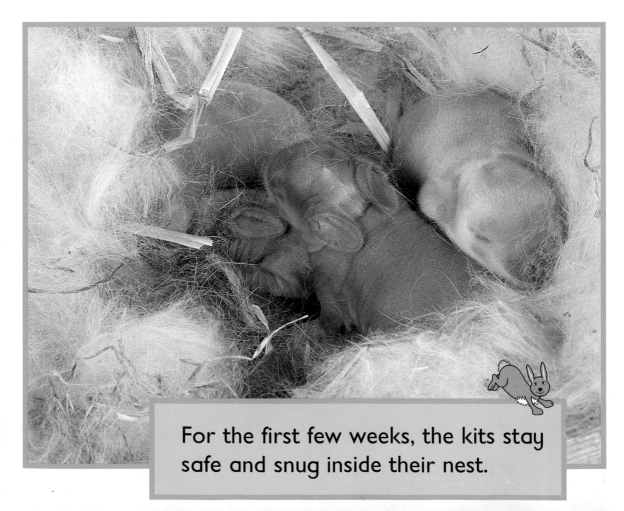

For the first few weeks, the kits stay safe and snug inside their nest.

The kits are old enough to leave their mother when they are about five weeks old. Then they are ready to become pet rabbits.

Rabbits can have lots of babies. It is best not to let them **breed**.

Your Pet Rabbits

Rabbits are fun to keep as pets, but they need lots of care. You must learn to look after your rabbit properly.

Rabbits are very friendly and love to be stroked.

When you go away on vacation, ask a friend to take care of your rabbit. Write a list of what your friend should do for the rabbit. Be sure to include the number of your pet's **veterinarian.**

Your rabbits need fresh food and water every day.

Choosing Your Rabbits

Animal shelters are often looking for good homes for rabbits. You can also buy rabbits from pet stores or from rabbit **breeders.**

Rabbits can get lonely. If you decide to have two rabbits, it is best to keep two **neutered** female rabbits together.

Choose a rabbit that looks healthy and lively. It should have a glossy coat, clear, bright eyes, and clean teeth.

This rabbit is healthy and ready to go to a good home.

Your Rabbits's Home

Your rabbits need a roomy cage to live in. The rabbit cage should have two rooms— one to live in and one for sleeping.

Do not use a cage with a wire bottom. The wire will hurt your rabbit's paws.

Line the bottom of the cage with newspaper.
Cover it with unscented wood **shavings.** A pile
of shredded paper or straw makes a cozy bed.

Rabbits stay much healthier
and live longer if they never
go outside.

Welcome Home

You can take your rabbit home in a strong carrying box. Be sure that the box has air holes in it so that your rabbit can breathe.

Rabbits will need some time alone to explore their new home.

Always pick up your rabbit properly. With one hand, gently grasp the scruff of its neck. Put your other arm around its bottom. Then lift it up.

Hold your rabbit close to your body to support its weight.

Playing With Your Rabbits

Rabbits need plenty of exercise. Make a room in the house that is safe for them to play in.

Do not let your rabbits get near electric, telephone, or computer power cords.

When they are out of their cage, keep your rabbits in the safe room. Do not let other animals in the room with your rabbits.

Play with your rabbits every day.
Otherwise, they will get bored.

Feeding Time

Pet stores sell special food pellets for rabbits. Rabbits also like to nibble on raw fruit and vegetables, such as lettuce, carrots, apples, and dandelion leaves.

Rabbits also like cabbage, broccoli, turnips, and parsley.

Feed your rabbits two small meals a day, one in the morning and one in the evening. Put the food in a heavy bowl that your rabbits cannot tip over.

Rabbits should have hay and water available at all times.

Cleaning the Cage

Rabbits are clean animals and do not like to live in a dirty cage. Remove wet bedding and **droppings** every day to keep your rabbit's cage clean.

Wash out the food bowls and water bottle every day.

Once a week, sweep the cage out. Every few weeks, wash it with warm, soapy water. Make sure that it is dry before you put your rabbits back in.

Always wash your hands after cleaning out your rabbit's cage.

Growing Up

Some rabbits grow very large. When you choose a rabbit, ask how big it will grow. Large rabbits need more space than small or medium-sized rabbits.

You might need to get a bigger rabbit cage as your rabbits grow up.

The sounds and movements your rabbits make are their way of talking. Rabbits twitch their noses to smell other rabbits and tell if they are friends.

Rabbits stamp their back feet if they are angry or frightened.

Healthy Rabbits

You should check with a **veterinarian** if your rabbits look sick. A runny nose and eyes, a dirty bottom, or not eating may be signs of sickness.

The veterinarian will examine your rabbits for signs of sickness or **disease.**

If your rabbit starts scratching a lot, it might have fleas. Check its fur, especially around its neck, for tiny, dark specks. These are flea **droppings.**

Ask an adult to use flea powder on your rabbit's fur to kill the fleas. Keeping your pet indoors will keep it from getting fleas.

Old Age

If you look after your rabbits, they may live for up to ten or twelve years. Take your rabbits to the **veterinarian** every six months for a checkup to make sure they stay healthy.

Make sure that your rabbits get plenty of exercise so that they do not gain weight.

Older rabbits need the same care as young rabbits. They should be given fresh food and water every day. Your rabbit will still like to be played with and stroked.

Caring for your rabbits will help you learn how to treat animals properly.

Useful Tips

- Give your rabbit a wooden block and cardboard toys to **gnaw** on to stop their front teeth from getting too long.

- Your rabbit may need its claws clipped from time to time. A **veterinarian** can do this for you.

- Rabbits **groom** themselves to keep their fur clean. But you need to brush long-haired rabbits, like angoras, every day. You can brush short-haired rabbits once a week.

- It is not a good idea to keep a rabbit with a guinea pig.

- All female rabbits need to be **neutered** to stay healthy and stop them from having babies.

Fact File

- Wild rabbits are small and brown. They live in large groups. Their homes are underground **burrows,** called warrens.

- Rabbits were first kept as pets about 400 years ago.

- There are about 100 different **breeds** of rabbits. The largest kind of pet rabbit is the Flemish giant. It is about the size of a small dog.

- Dwarf rabbits are the smallest kind. They can weigh less than a bag of sugar.

- Lop-eared rabbits have the longest ears. They can grow longer than your arm.

Glossary

animal shelter place where lost or unwanted animals live until they are given new homes

breed type or kind of an animal

breeder someone who raises animals

burrow hole or tunnel in the ground

disease sickness

dropping waste from the body

gnaw chew and bite

groom gently brush and clean your rabbit's fur. Rabbits also groom themselves.

litter group of baby rabbits

neutered when a rabbit has an operation so that it cannot have any babies

shaving thin slice or strip of wood

veterinarian doctor who cares for animals

More Books to Read

An older reader can help you with these books.

Carroll, David. *The ASPCA Complete Guide to Pet Care.* New York: Dutton/Plume, 2001.

Klingel, Cynthia Fitterer, and Robert B. Noyed. *Rabbits.* Eden Prairie, Minn.: The Child's World, Incorporated, 2000.

Miller, Michaela. *Rabbits.* Chicago: Heinemann Library, 1998.

Mitchell, Melanie S. *Rabbits.* Minneapolis, Minn.: Lerner Publishing Group, 2002.

Whitehouse, Patricia. *Rabbits.* Chicago: Heinemann Library, 2003.

A Note from the ASPCA™

Pets are often our good friends for the very best of reasons. They don't care how we look, how we dress, or who our friends are. They like us because we are nice to them and take care of them. That's what being friends is all about.

This book has given you information to help you know what your pet needs. Learn all you can from this book and others, and from people who know about animals, such as veterinarians and workers at animal shelters like the ASPCA™. You will soon become your pet's most important friend.

Index